TPS SURPLUS

HAMMER

2 LEGIT 2 QUIT

HAMMER
2 LEGIT 2 QUIT

BY

LINDA SAYLOR-MARCHANT

DILLON PRESS
New York

Maxwell Macmillan Canada
Toronto
Maxwell Macmillan International
New York   Oxford   Singapore   Sydney

For my parents, Violet and Waymond, who instilled in me the difference between right and wrong and the importance of being a positive role model. To my husband and children, Garth Sr., Aziza, Eleanor, and Garth Jr., whom I cherish so dearly; and to Elaine, who was very instrumental in helping me to begin another fruitful career.

Photo Credits

Front Cover: Michael Benabib/Retna Pictures, Ltd.
Back Cover: Gary Gershoff/Retna Pictures, Ltd.

Retna Pictures, Ltd.: Eddie Maluk (2); Steve Granitz (5, 12, 20, 30, 45, 48, 52, 58); Carraro/Stills (6); Larry Busacca (9); Frank Micelotta (15, 33); Justin Thomas (18, 49); S. Thomann (22, 39); Adrian Green (24); Michael Putland (28, 35); Gary Gershoff (41); Fitzroy Barrett (42); Lori Stoll (50); Barry Talesnick (56)

Library of Congress Cataloging-in-Publication Data

Saylor-Marchant, Linda
    Hammer / by Linda Saylor-Marchant.—1st ed.
      p.   cm. — (Taking part)
    Includes index.
    Summary: A biography of the popular musician known as M. C. Hammer, who was the first rap performer to reach the top of the Billboard Hot 100.
    ISBN 0-87518-522-3
    1. Hammer, M. C., 1963- —Juvenile literature. 2. Rap musicians—United States—Biography—Juvenile literature.
[1. Hammer, M. C., 1963- . 2. Rap musicians. 3. Entertainers. 4. Afro-Americans—Biography.] I. Title. II. Series.
ML3930.H18S4 1992
782.42164—dc20   [B]   92-4412

Dillon Press
Macmillan Publishing Company
866 Third Avenue
New York, NY 10022

Maxwell Macmillan Canada, Inc.
1200 Eglinton Avenue East
Suite 200
Don Mills, Ontario M3C 3N1

Macmillan Publishing Company is part of the Maxwell Communication Group of Companies

First edition
Printed in the United States of America
    10 9 8 7 6 5 4 3 2 1

Contents

INTRODUCTION

He's one of the hippest, sexiest rap artists ever to hit the music scene. He is best known for his fancy footwork, his colorful wardrobe, and his "posse," the group of dancers that performs along with him. Right now he is enjoying phenomenal success, mostly due to sales of his megahit albums *Please Hammer Don't Hurt 'Em*, which contains the smash hits "U Can't Touch This" and "Pray," and *Too Legit to Quit*, which is burning up the charts with songs like the title track.

Who is this young superstar? None other than Hammer, the man who is getting the credit for taking rap music in a whole new direction. Thanks to this talented performer, more and more people who had never been exposed to rap are developing a taste for this hot new music form. And behind Hammer's hip-swerving, hand-waving beat is a moral message that offers hope and encouragement.

Hammer's ability to appeal to many different audiences has made him a star.

HAMMER 2 LEGIT 2 QUIT

Hammer's talents extend far beyond just rapping. He is also a choreographer, promoter, producer, actor, and businessperson. He is a husband and a father. He is an energetic dancer who swirls across a stage like a tornado. His genie pants and tank tops reveal a muscular, fit body, his arms and legs continuously pump to a funky beat.

This amazing performer is the first to bring rap music to a mainstream audience including African Americans, Hispanics, Asians, and whites from all walks of life. His fans love him. Even some people who aren't fans of rap music have found something good to say about Hammer. One music critic remarked, "I hate rap music, but I love M. C. Hammer."

Not everyone loves him. Some critics have called him merely a good dancer with nothing to say who made it big. Yet others describe him as a musical genius, the "Michael Jackson of rap." Whether they love him or hate him, most people agree that Hammer is one of the most popular performers of the hottest sound in music.

Everyone is talking about rap music's funky sound,

Hammer and fellow rapper Vanilla Ice

its raw lyrics, and its flashy artists. But rap isn't really all that new. It has been around for over a decade; it just wasn't played on many radio stations. Until recently, most popular music stations played rock, country, or rhythm and blues. If rap music was played at all, it was on the radio stations devoted mostly to rhythm and blues.

Now, thanks to artists such as Hammer, Salt-N-Pepa, L. L. Cool J, and Queen Latifah, rap music has made its way onto mainstream radio and MTV, and it is now one of the most popular types of music around.

HAMMER 2 LEGIT 2 QUIT

This sudden popularity didn't happen overnight. It took many years of hard work and persistence by early rap artists to keep rap music alive. Kurtis Blow, Grandmaster Flash, Melle Mel, and the Sugar Hill Gang are a few of the early pioneers who dedicated their careers to getting rap established. Their determination and talent inspired others to follow in their footsteps.

Rap developed in the late 1970s in the ghettos of New York and Los Angeles. Its audience was mainly the people who lived in these communities—mostly African Americans and Hispanics, with a few whites. Rap's lyrics are about life on the streets and the problems suffered by many of the people who live in the ghettos: drugs, crime, unemployment, and feelings of oppression. The lyrics are simply spoken to a beat, with the performer telling a story over the music.

At first most rappers were men. Today, there are many women, such as M.C. Lyte and Yo Yo performing rap songs that tell women's stories.

Although the new sound of rap was considered in its early days hip, it was a risk that the big record companies avoided. To record company executives, rap music seemed to be a big investment that didn't guarantee any profits. Some people thought rap was just a passing fad that would fade quickly. The idea that a rapper could become a worldwide sensation was inconceivable to most music industry people.

After being turned down by the big music labels, some of the early rappers decided to form their own record label devoted to rap and other musical forms that had a hard time finding their place in the mainstream. This new record label was called Sugar Hill Records. Sylvia, a sultry singer popular in the 1970s, played an instrumental part in organizing this bold new company, which gave many rappers their first big breaks in show business.

With the creation of Sugar Hill, rap was on its way to becoming an accepted part of the music world. But it would take many years and a lot of hard work before a rap artist would be in the number one spot on the *Billboard* Hot 100.

FROM BATBOY TO RAP KING

Stanley Kirk Burrell, known today simply as Hammer, was born on March 30, 1963, in east Oakland, California, before rap music was even beginning. Like many African Americans who are successful today, Stanley was not born into wealth. He came from a very large family and was the youngest of seven children. His parents worked hard day and night to support their family. His father, Louis Burrell, Sr., managed a neighborhood social club called The Oaks. His mother worked at various jobs, including one in the criminal division of the Oakland Police Department.

Like most children, Stanley loved listening to music and dreamed of developing his talent and being a star. Even at the age of three he began making up dances to go with the music. But these dances were more than just childish games. Young Stanley was serious about his hobby and wanted to develop his talent.

Hammer's experience as a batboy paid off when he faced Dwight Gooden during MTV's Rock N' Jock softball game.

Today, when reporters ask Hammer when he started dancing, he always replies, "I've been dancing ever since I was born."

Stanley's first performances took place at home, with his brothers and sisters as his audience. James Brown, the Godfather of Soul, was Stanley's idol, and young Stanley loved to imitate him. Hammer remembers doing the whole routine of the James Brown hit "Please, Please, Please" for his family. While his brother took a sheet or towel and laid it over Stanley's back as a cape, the young performer would fall to the ground and crawl across the floor—just like James Brown did in his shows.

As Stanley got older, his imitations got better. He began to attract audiences other than family members. He decided to take his Godfather of Soul routine out of the living room and onto the streets.

During the summer Stanley would perform his routine in the parking lot of the Oakland Coliseum, home of the Oakland A's baseball team. People enjoyed watching the show. The crowd of onlookers, mainly baseball fans going in and out of the stadium for the games, grew

Hammer performs with James Brown, whose routines he imitated as a boy.

larger each time he performed. Soon, Stanley's parking lot performances became the talk of the stadium. Word got around to the A's owner, Charlie Finley. He became curious about this unofficial opening act that everyone was talking about.

One afternoon Finley decided to come out of his executive office for some fresh air. While walking around the parking lot, he noticed a group of fans watching something and cheering loudly. The game hadn't started yet, so he knew it couldn't be the baseball team.

As Finley approached the crowd, he noticed Stanley

dancing nonstop, swirling around the lot, performing splits and other hot moves. Finley realized that this was the kid everyone was talking about, and he stayed to watch. Stanley was so caught up in his James Brown routine that he didn't even notice Finley watching him from the sidelines.

After the performance was over, Finley walked up and introduced himself to Stanley. Then he made the 11-year-old boy a surprising offer: He invited Stanley to come watch the baseball game from the owner's box. The excited young performer couldn't believe it—he was going to watch the A's play, and he was going to see it all from the best seat in the stadium!

After the game, Finley offered the energetic boy a job as the A's errand boy. Stanley accepted, and soon he was running errands for the team. This was a great job for an 11-year-old, and he loved it. He worked hard and was eventually promoted to official batboy for the A's.

As the batboy, Stanley often traveled with the team. This experience was very valuable for him. He learned that the world was much bigger than just Oakland,

California, and that there were exciting new people and places outside of his hometown.

Stanley was well liked by the players on the Oakland A's and on the teams they played. One day Pedro Garcia, who was playing with the Milwaukee Brewers, noticed Stanley's resemblance to baseball legend "Hammerin'" Hank Aaron. Pedro mentioned this to the other team players. Soon the word spread among the entire baseball community that Stanley resembled Hank. Home run hitter Reggie Jackson started calling Stanley "Hammer." The nickname caught on, and pretty soon little Stanley became known as Hammer, the name he would use from then on.

Hammer moved up quickly in the A's organization. Whenever Finley was out of town, Hammer gave the owner a play-by-play report of the games over the phone in the executive offices. During the late 1970s, the A's were performing poorly, partly because they traded away a few key players like Reggie Jackson and Catfish Hunter. The A's staff began to dwindle as well, and because of this, Hammer had the opportunity to move

An athlete since he was very young, Hammer still enjoys an active lifestyle.

18

up. Charlie Finley jokingly gave him the title of "executive vice president," and gave him a salary of $7.50 per game. Even though Hammer wasn't really an executive, he did get to enjoy one benefit: He got to sit in the owner's box for every game.

The young Hammer, influenced by his baseball job, now dreamed of playing professional baseball. Charlie Finley often told Hammer, "I can't promise that you're going to be a professional baseball player, but I can say you will make a positive contribution to your race. You're going to be somebody of importance."

Hammer respected Charlie Finley's opinions, but at the time he was convinced that professional baseball was his future. Even so, Hammer did not neglect his other interests. He enjoyed school and was both smart and popular. To Hammer, going to school meant being a well-rounded individual, not someone who focused on just one aspect of life.

Hammer also concentrated on perfecting his dancing. Whenever there was a school talent show, he performed for his classmates. He often stole the show, dazzling his

Although he traded his glove for a mike, Hammer still enjoys throwing a ball around on the field.

audience with explosive moves.

After graduating from high school, Hammer attended a local college in Oakland, where he majored in communications. While in college, he also pursued his dream of becoming a professional baseball player. With his experience with the A's and his years as a second baseman in high school, he felt that he could easily make it in the pros. However, when Hammer tried out for the San Francisco Giants, he didn't make the team. This was a big disappointment to him because baseball was such an important part of his life.

Upset over being rejected by the Giants, Hammer decided to drop out of college. Now he faced the most important decision of his life. Without the backing of an education, there were two roads he could take: the dead-end path followed by many of the young people in his community or the road that would take him to his musical success.

Many of the "homeboys" in Hammer's neighborhood wore the latest designer clothes, drove fancy cars, and had several beautiful girlfriends. They always had money to spend, and they never seemed to work. Hammer knew that some of these young men made between $5,000 and $6,000 a week. And he knew that all he had to do to join them was do what they did—sell drugs.

But Hammer rejected the life-style of the pushers. He knew that he wanted to do something positive with his life, and he knew that selling or taking drugs, no matter how much money it would make him, would only be a dead end.

Turning his back on the drug scene, Hammer began looking for some direction in his life. So in the early 1980s

Hammer's positive attitude helped him avoid the temptations of life on the streets.

a young man with little money or experience. But two men in particular knew that Hammer would be an excellent long-term investment. They were Dwayne Murphy and Mike Davis, who played for the Oakland A's and knew Hammer from his days as a batboy there. Both men decided to invest $20,000 apiece in Hammer's music career. Shortly afterward the men took out a $125,000 bank loan on Hammer's behalf.

With these generous investments and the business skills he had learned while working for the A's, Hammer launched his new label, Bustin' Records. He was able to complete his debut single, "Ring 'Em." The record was sold out of the trunk of his car.

Since his music career seemed to be moving along well, Hammer decided to form a group of singers and dancers to perform with him. This new addition to his act was called his "posse." It consisted of a bodyguard and three female singers called Oaktown's 3-5-7. Oaktown's 3-5-7 spent tireless hours rehearsing their singing and dancing routines. Sweet L.D., one of Oaktown's 3-5-7, described their rehearsals like this: "We danced thirteen

Hammer and his posse burn up the stage.

or fourteen hours a day, the same routine over and over again, from Sunday to Sunday."

Those rehearsals were rough, but they would help make Hammer's posse one of the most respected organizations in the music business.

THE BIG TIME

"Ring 'Em" was Hammer's first release, but certainly not his last. After wrapping up that record, he started producing a new single called "Let's Get It Started." This time he didn't do it alone. He teamed up with a professional producer named Felton Pilate. Pilate and Hammer worked in a makeshift studio, recording and mixing the single.

During these rehearsals, Hammer compiled songs for his first album, *Feel My Power*. Released in 1987, *Feel My Power* sold 66,000 copies, a good showing for a record released without any major-label backing. Most of the record's success was due to Hammer's wife, Stephanie. She promoted the album by taking copies to radio stations and DJs at popular clubs in the San Francisco Bay area and asking them to play it.

Hammer was now well on his way to success. One night in 1988, while he and his posse were performing at the Oak Tree Cabaret, they were spotted by a talent

Hammer walks away with an armload of American Music Awards.

scout from Capitol Records. The scout invited them to audition in Los Angeles. Record company executives were so impressed with the audition that Capitol signed Hammer to a record contract and gave him a $750,000 advance to begin work on his next album. They also rereleased *Feel My Power* under a new title, *Let's Get It Started*. This time the record went platinum, selling over 1.5 million copies.

In the meantime, Hammer went on tour to promote his records. His second album was recorded in the back of the tour bus, while the band traveled from show to show. Titled *Please Hammer Don't Hurt Em*, it was released in 1989. Thanks to the success of the smash hit single "U Can't Touch This," the album sold over five million copies in its first year of release and remained at the top of the *Billboard* Hot 100 for 18 weeks. It was the first rap record ever to reach the number one position.

During an interview, Hammer said, "When I make a record, I hope that everybody will like the song, whether they're black or white. In the case of 'U Can't Touch This,' I thought of that phrase and thought

Hammer's live shows bring his fans to their feet.

it sounded like a hit."

With the phenomenal success of *Please Hammer Don't Hurt Em*, Hammer suddenly was a superstar. And unlike many other rap artists, he found that his music appealed to people of all backgrounds, classes, and colors.

Much of M. C. Hammer's success has to do with his live shows. His 1990 show in Tokyo sold over 55,000 tickets in under six hours! That is unusual for rap music concerts. Hammer stands apart from acts such as NWA or Public Enemy, who rap solely about issues that affect African Americans. Hammer raps about issues faced by all kinds of people.

Hammer's ability to appeal to audiences of all races is due in large part to his dynamic performing style. He is not a typical rapper, because he sings and dances as well. Most rappers confine themselves to simply rapping, lip-synching while a DJ "scratches" on two turntables. The rappers walk back and forth across the stage, microphone in hand, rapping about black life or about other rappers. They usually wear plain clothes— sweatsuits, hats, sneakers—and big gold chains.

The lyrics of Hammer's songs are very important to him.

But Hammer believes that a show should be just that—a real show. He wears bright clothes and stages elaborate dance numbers to go with his music. His dancers race around the stage with him, dressed in colorful costumes. Often there are as many as 30 people on stage at once!

When asked why he goes to so much trouble to delight his fans, Hammer says, "You might as well put on the record [of most rap artists] or watch the video, because at 90 percent of these concerts, the rap artists are actually doing a 'putting on the hits' when they perform." They are lip-synching to their record and not giving the fans a live show.

Hammer speaks from personal experience. When he started out, he, too, lip-synched to tapes because he couldn't afford all the equipment needed to perform live. At one show he admitted to his fans, "I'm not even doing the whole song." Hammer didn't feel good about himself after these shows. He felt he was doing his fans an injustice by just playing a record and moving around the stage.

Today Hammer's performances are high tech and his music is always live. Hammer says he gets his inspiration from the live shows he saw when he was a young boy—shows given by such classic acts as his hero, James Brown, and groups like Earth, Wind, and Fire. When he was growing up, Hammer once said, "If I ever become famous, I will really put on a show."

Hammer also owes a lot of his success to fans who see his show and tell their friends to go. "It has spread through word of mouth and through the media that it's the most entertaining show out there," he says happily.

Now that Hammer has found mainstream success, he has come under attack from some of the more traditional, hard-core rappers. They accuse him of not getting the message of African Americans across. They say he has forgotten about life on the streets and in the ghetto.

Some critics have even questioned the religious message of his hit single "Pray," saying that it doesn't offer realistic answers to today's problems. The song, which has a very positive message for young people trying to make it today, differs greatly from the lyrics of more hard-core rappers like Ice-T, Ice Cube, or Public Enemy. Where these groups complain about the problems of crime and drugs, Hammer offers positive solutions. He believes that rather than get angry and complain, people should look for ways to change their lives for the better.

Hammer doesn't worry about the so-called rap standards or how others feel about him. He says, "If they had their way, they would keep rap in a small box only for the hard-core inner-city people. They think anytime the public at large embraces rap, then it's no good. They have been making negative comments about me since day one, but they knew in their minds that they couldn't trash me."

Hammer does have some support from the hard-core rappers. Chuck D of Public Enemy called Hammer his favorite rapper. Ice-T, the hard-core rapper from Los Angeles, says that Hammer "is cool, but he's not hip-hop."

Hammer has also been criticized by some reporters for the strict, military-style way he handles members of his posse during rehearsals and while they are on the road. But Hammer defends his management style. "We run a clean organization and a very disciplined operation," he says. "There are members in my group that are still teenagers and I feel very responsible for them. We allow them to grow up, but we try to maintain a very positive organization and keep everybody out of trouble."

Hammer just shrugs off the negative press. "I can take the heat. My background on the streets of Oakland made me thick-skinned and able to take the potshots from the media."

Hammer's fans obviously aren't bothered by the bad

THE MUSIC AND THE MESSAGE

Most of Hammer's songs sound familiar when you first hear them. This is because many of them contain pieces of songs that were hits once before, often during the early 1970s through the early 1980s. It is a very common practice for rap artists to use music created by other performers. Sometimes the original artist gets a songwriting credit on the new song, and may even be paid royalties (part of the money earned from sales of the record) from the new song.

The practice of taking bits of old music and using them to create a new sound is called sampling. Although sampling is a very common practice in the rap music world, not everyone is happy about it. The rock group Queen and singer David Bowie recently won a sampling lawsuit against rapper Vanilla Ice. The rapper had used long pieces from their hit song "Pressure" as part of his number one smash "Ice, Ice Baby," without

Performing live is Hammer's biggest thrill.

crediting any of the writers.

Hammer also uses sampling, but he is careful to get permission from the artists that he samples. The funky beat behind Hammer's chart-topping hit "U Can't Touch This" is actually a part of funk legend Rick James's hit song "Super Freak." Hammer paid James for the use of his song and credited him in the album's liner notes. When Hammer and James met face-to-face for the first time, backstage at the Buffalo Memorial Auditorium, Hammer got to thank his hero in person.

"I used to go to your concerts," Hammer told James. "I felt good using music from a person I idolized. Y'all used to come out and do a show. Then I'd do my thing at the club to 'Super Freak.'"

James was pleased to hear this and told Hammer, "Keep doing it!" The two have agreed to work together on a project in the future.

Hammer also used sampling on his second hit, "Pray." This time he got help from Prince's great song "When Doves Cry." Though the song was originally a soulful ballad, Hammer took the melody and turned it

Hammer with his longtime idol James Brown

into a funky dance number. While you can still easily recognize Prince's music, "Pray" has a new sound that is totally Hammer's. That is typical of Hammer: He enjoys letting his favorite artists know that their music influenced him, but his own style comes through to show that he is still in control of what he does.

Another song on *Please Hammer Don't Hurt 'Em* samples Motown legend Marvin Gaye's song "Mercy Mercy Me" as part of Hammer's "Help the Children." Hammer also re-creates the Chi-Lites ballad "Have You Seen Her" as a rap number. The Chi-Lites were very happy that another artist liked their 1971 hit enough to bring it back to life. After hearing the new version, they called Hammer to thank him for reviving their record.

But Hammer's music isn't important just because of the artists he samples. There is a message behind the funky beat, and that message is positive and hopeful. His songs are not just about dancing and having a good time. Instead, they are intended to make people—especially young people—think.

Drug abuse is something Hammer has long been

concerned about, and "Help the Children" contains an anti-drug statement. Part of the proceeds from the song go to a foundation for needy children. And "Pray" is Hammer's way of saying that he believes in a higher power that can help us make it through the struggles we face every day.

The themes in both songs, Hammer says, are messages from him to his daughter, Akeiba. "It is important that her father set a positive example, that his songs contain lyrics that mean something," he says, talking of the responsibility he feels. "I try to stay very real, very much in touch. I don't want to be self-righteous. I never profess to be a perfect person, because I'm not."

Regarding drugs, and why he works so hard to get his anti-drug message heard, Hammer has this to say: "Drugs is the problem that I'm closest to. I'm trying to create awareness among those who are using drugs that their lives can be shortened."

Hammer's talents extend far beyond creating great music. He is also a songwriter, producer, choreographer, and record company executive. When he's not on the

Hammer and his daughter, Akeiba

Hammer works out to stay in shape.

road, he attends baseball and football games and other sporting events. He also spends as much time as he can at home with his wife and little girl.

Another of Hammer's passions is exercise. His energetic stage shows require that he stay in great shape, so Hammer runs every day. Before shows, he performs 300 sit-ups and lifts weights to keep his body toned. His legs are so important to him that he recently took out an insurance policy on them. "Many athletes

Hammer performs one of his original dance moves.

have policies in case they get injured on or off the field," he explains. "If they can't continue their playing careers, they get a certain amount of money. I have the same policy."

Hammer not only exercises; he eats right. His daily diet consists of chicken and fresh fruit. He also drinks about ten quarts of orange juice every day!

All of this dieting and exercise seems to have paid off. Hammer's body is considered one of the sexiest in show business, and his fans' reactions when he comes on stage confirms this. How does Hammer handle it when his fans get too close? Does he actually tell them "You Can't Touch This"? Hammer says it isn't a problem. He says that he was with his wife, Stephanie, long before he was ever Hammer the star and that they are very much in love.

Not a lot is known about Hammer's personal life, and he wants to keep it that way. "It is hard for me to have a private life," he complains. "Once you lose your privacy, you know what it is to have it, so I'm going to let my wife and daughter maintain their privacy."

TOO LEGIT TO QUIT

After the success of *Please Hammer Don't Hurt 'Em*, everyone wondered what Hammer would do next. Would he be a one-hit-wonder and never produce another good record, or would he make something even better?

When Hammer's second album hit the stores in 1991, everyone was in for a big surprise. Titled *Too Legit to Quit*, the album was another first in rap music: All of the music on the album was original! Not one song on the album contains sampling. No rapper had ever released a record without sampling before.

The second album reflected another change in Hammer's life. He announced that he had dropped the M.C. from his name. From now on, he wanted to be called just Hammer.

"Too Legit to Quit" was the first single from the new album, and it was a smash. Not only was the song a hit, the video that accompanied it was a favorite as well. In

Hammer smiles for the crowd before performing on the MTV Music Video Awards.

it, Hammer is joined by his longtime hero, James Brown. Hammer was thrilled to be able to perform with the man he used to imitate when he was a little boy.

Hammer also released a song called "Addams Groove," the theme song from the hit movie *The Addams Family*. It, too, was a favorite on radio and MTV.

Hammer is always looking forward. He knows that he can't be a hot performer forever, so he prepares for the future by expanding his career into areas besides rapping.

Hammer does much of his planning and work at his huge San Francisco estate. Reflecting his phenomenal success, it has a recording studio, a rehearsal hall, a media room, and a gym. There are also two swimming pools, a reflecting pool, and a nine-car garage. On any given day, musicians and dancers from the posse can be found practicing in the rehearsal hall or relaxing by the pool.

Besides working with the posse, Hammer is involved in producing different groups through Bust It Productions, the company he created. Some of the artists he is currently working with are the group Special Generation, rappers One Cause and Effect, and hip-hop singer B Angie B.

Hammer is also in demand as a spokesperson for different companies and products. He can be seen in commercials for Taco Bell and British Knights footwear. His song "U Can't Touch This" was the anthem for the Detroit Pistons, the 1991 National Basketball Association champions. His Hammertime T-shirts sold like hotcakes during the NBA finals. Mattel, the toy company famous for creating the Barbie and Ken dolls, has even come out with a Hammer doll that moves like the real thing.

In 1990, Hammer signed a deal with Pepsi-Cola in which he agreed to endorse their soft drink. They in turn would sponsor his tour. Hammer was also the spokesperson for Pepsi's 1990-1991 National School Assembly program. As part of this program, he went around the country speaking to school groups about the dangers of drugs and the importance of education. John Moorhead, a Pepsi executive, said that "Hammer

A group of young fans helps Hammer promote the Hammer doll.

speaks a message worth promoting—that our society needs to focus its energies on nurturing and educating children."

Hammer also works to bring a positive message to children every Saturday morning on television. No, he doesn't have his own talk show—he is the star of a cartoon series, *Hammerman*, for ABC. The cartoon hero Hammerman has special powers, which he gets from a pair of magic dancing shoes. Hammer is very proud of the show, which he helps to supervise. The first episode focused on graffiti and having respect for other people's property. Hammer's message: "It is wrong to mark on other people's property. Instead, make your mark in society doing something positive. Who knows? You might end up drawing cartoons for television."

While Hammer has been busy with his interests, some of his family members have invested in a different business—thoroughbred horse racing. Hammer's brother Louis, Jr., who is also his manager, always wanted to own a stable. Now, with Hammer's

Hammer takes a break before a show.

help, the dream is a reality. Along with Hammer's father, Louis, Sr., they own and operate Oaktown Stables. They have 17 prize racehorses.

Louis, Sr., and Louis, Jr., have named several of their horses in honor of their famous family member. One is called Hammerman, another is called Dance Floor, and a third answers to Rap Master.

So what else is left for Hammer to do? He has already appeared on talk shows such as the *Oprah Winfrey Show* and the *Arsenio Hall Show*. He also made his television acting debut on an episode of *Amen*, in which he played a dual role as himself and Reverend Pressure, a showy preacher with a fiery message. In the show, actor Bumper Robinson plays a student who is thinking of dropping out of high school to follow his dream of being a rap star. Hammer persuades him to finish his high-school education first.

It seems like Hammer has done everything there is to do. But he is sure to have more surprises in store for his fans. He is planning a tour to support *Too Legit to Quit*, and is already thinking about the songs for his next album. His drive and determination take him from one project to the next, and he doesn't show any signs of slowing down.

Feel My Power
Capitol Records, 1988

Please Hammer Don't Hurt 'Em
Capitol Records, 1989

Too Legit to Quit
Capitol Records, 1991

VIDEO COLLECTIONS

U Can't Touch This
Capitol, 1989

Pray
Capitol, 1989

Save the Children
Capitol, 1989

Too Legit to Quit
Capitol Records, 1991

Do Not Pass Me By
Capitol, 1991

I n D E X

Linda Saylor-Marchant lives with her husband and three children in Queens, New York. She is a freelance writer and librarian at the Queens Library—Laurelton Branch. She holds a bachelor's degree in business administration from York College and a master's degree in library science from the University of Pittsburgh.